ML
647.9577 H121
c.1
Hagen, Jeff.
Fry me to the moon /

P9-DEF-817

Fry Me to the Moon

WITHDRAWN

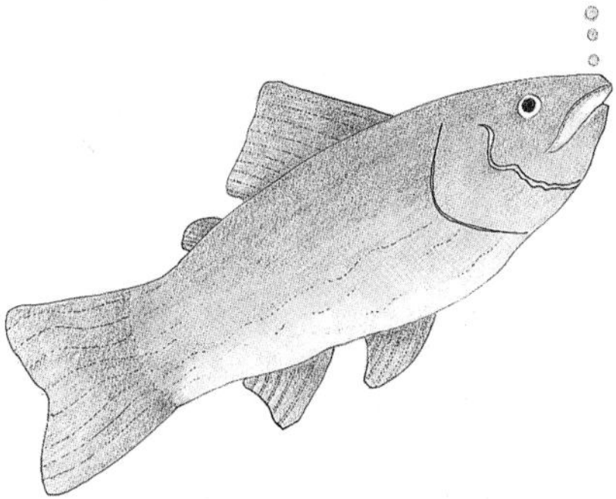

Other books by Jeff Hagen

Hiawatha Passing

Steeple Chase

Northern Retreats

Fry Me to the Moon

Text and drawings by
Jeff Hagen

Prairie Oak Press
Madison, Wisconsin

First edition, first printing

Copyright © 1999 by Jeff Hagen

All rights reserved. No part of this publication may be reproduced or transmitted in any form or by any means, electronic or mechanical, including photocopy, recording, or any information storage or retrieval system, without permission in writing from the publisher.

Prairie Oak Press
821 Prospect Place
Madison, Wisconsin 53703

Typeset by Quick Quality Press, Madison, Wisconsin

Cover Design by Flying Fish Graphics, Blue Mounds, Wisconsin

Printed in Korea

ISBN 1-879483-58-0

FOND DU LAC PUBLIC LIBRARY

647.9577
H121

Dedicated to my son, Kit

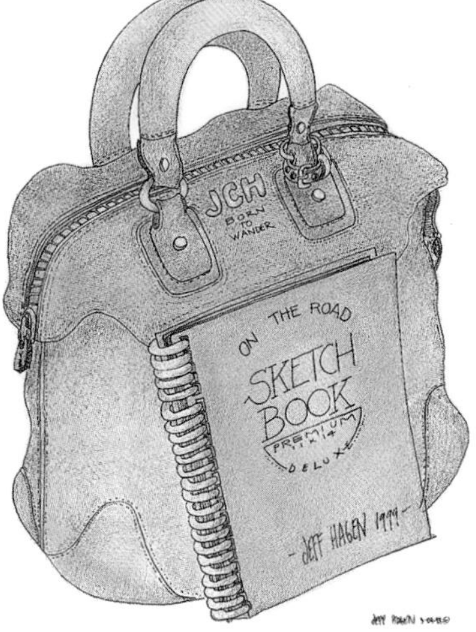

1-6-00 3.82 City

FOND DU LAC PUBLIC LIBRARY

Contents

Acknowledgments

A very special thank you to Bonnie Berens, David Personius, Father Bud Hollander, Doug Edmunds, Angel Travis, Lorene Carter, Bob Grieves, Dennis McCann, Jerry Minnich, Kristin Visser, Ron Trimberger, Lyn Jefferson, and Dave and Connie Shoemaker for all their help, advice, and support in making this creative endeavor a reality.

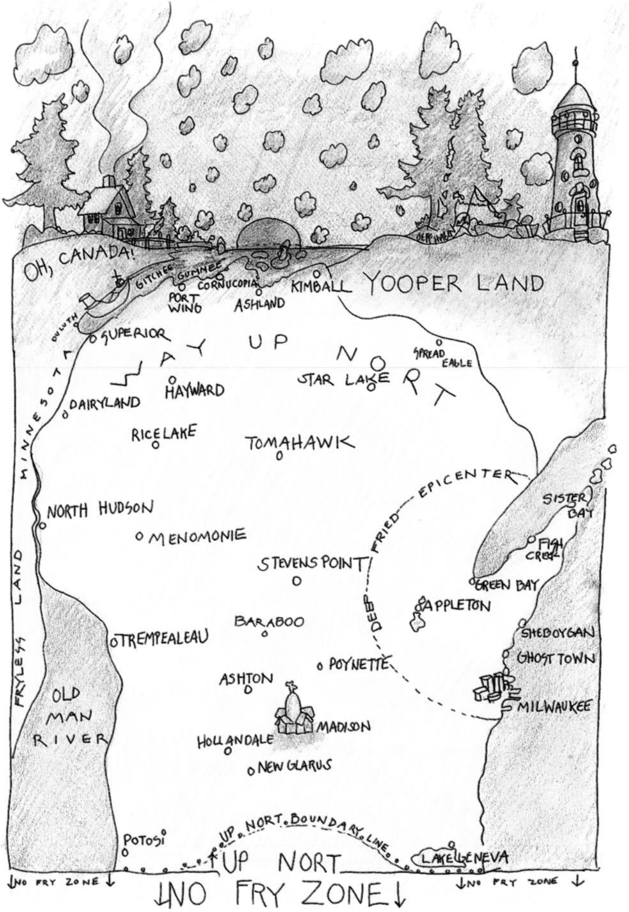
OH, CANADA!
GITCHEE GUMMEE
CORNUCOPIA
PORT WING
ASHLAND
KIMBALL
YOOPER LAND
DULUTH
SUPERIOR
WAY UP NORT
SPREAD EAGLE
STAR LAKE
HAYWARD
DAIRYLAND
MINNESOTA
RICE LAKE
TOMAHAWK
EPICENTER
DEEP FRIED
SISTER BAY
NORTH HUDSON
MENOMONIE
FISH CREEK
STEVENS POINT
GREEN BAY
APPLETON
FRYLESS LAND
BARABOO
TREMPEALEAU
SHEBOYGAN
GHOST TOWN
POYNETTE
ASHTON
OLD MAN RIVER
MILWAUKEE
MADISON
HOLLANDALE
NEW GLARUS
POTOSI
UP NORT BOUNDARY LINE
UP NORT
LAKE GENEVA
NO FRY ZONE
NO FRY ZONE
NO FRY ZONE

Introduction

Small Fry

This is a small book about a big institution in Wisconsin: The Friday night fish fry and beyond.

Within these pages, I visited a sampling of public eateries and seasonal fish fry events across the state that serve fish in one form or another to the hungry traveler.

I ventured out into Dairyland to seek and visit a variation of venues and locales.

Initially, I asked "official experts" for suggestions and leads to follow.

I asked food critics, tourist people, state officials, and others who would be in a position to know.

The results were disappointing, artificial, and promotionally tainted.

Before going any farther, I need to make the mission and purpose of this book clear.

This book doesn't claim to be a food review, critics choice, or "best" of anything.

Instead, this book is a lighthearted view of a cultural phenomenon which people in Wisconsin lovingly cherish.

Plain and simple, I was looking for places that didn't have pedigree or snobbery.

I was looking for the real places that serve up fish with a side order of good-natured fun.

Within these pages are places that go "beyond" the conventional fish fry. They offer creative departures in the form of grilled fish, broiled, blackened fish, and exotic variations.

Some places have "bones in-bones out" choices.

This initially puzzled me. I couldn't conceive of why someone would want "bones in!"

A cook in a little northern cafe gave me the answer.

"A lot of the people from the old country prefer bones in because it gives them added flavor, like a soup bone or roast marrow does."

As I ventured further into this journey, I found that it is a deep pond filled with a mixture of people's choices and traditions.

New fish swim with the habits of old generations.

I found entire families who had attended the same fish fry for over thirty years. I found places where fish came on a paper plate without knife or fork. I learned of one place that puts up a sign during their weekly fish fry that reads, "No coffee served during fish fry." When I asked why, the owner said, "Because people would linger too much and we need to get people in and out for others to eat."

There are some serious fish fry eaters out there! But, by and large, I found that they all shared one common denominator, whether it was in the small town of Cornucopia or in the big cities of Milwaukee, Madison, and Green Bay. That common denominator is fun on a Friday night shared in communal joy with others.

Frankly, I like swimming in that kind of common pool of humanity and good humor.

Come on in, the water's just fine.

Why a Fry?

On a gray rainy day in early summer, I pulled into a Wisconsin Welcome Center on Highway 12, just south of Pell Lake.

My mission was simple—to seek suggestions from the locals about a good fish fry in the area, and a starting point for this book.

I found several people in the center who were happy to recall their favorite places. During our conversation, two Harleys with California plates pulled up in front of the building.

The riders wore the unmistakable badge of the open road and a hard cross-country journey—tan skin and weather-beaten faces. They were on the last leg from L.A. to the colossal Harley Davidson Birthday Celebration in Milwaukee.

They stood there for a few moments watching us and catching the tail-end of our conversation. As I gathered up my notes and list of local hot spots for fish, one of the black-leathered West Coast nomads asked the question of us. "Excuse me, but what the hell is a fish fry?"

Indeed, what is a fish fry? A real fish fry?

What is this phenomenon, which is such an enigma to the rest of the world. And why is it such a big thing here?

I set out to learn why.

Why is this such a big deal in Wisconsin? Why do some people regard "it" as a religious ritual of the highest order?

Why does the almighty New York Times assign a reporter to write about this culinary-cultural event, unique and indigenous to the Dairy State?

Why do former Wisconsinites living outside the state actually drive back on Fridays to indulge in deep-fried delight?

I wanted to know, so I asked the people who run the fish fries—Catholic priests, supper club owners, chefs and cooks. Together they provided me with the answer.

There are four factors involved in the state legacy:

First is the ethnic and religious background of Wisconsin's population. It is largely German Catholic.

For years, meatless Fridays were the rule. Many churches and small bars nearby held Friday night fish fries for people of the faith.

This changed with the emergence of Vatican Two.

Second is Wisconsin's proximity to the Great Lakes. If you haven't noticed, we have two of them along our state borders. Up until the 1950s, both Lake Superior and Lake Michigan provided a cornucopia of fresh-water fish.

This home-based fish supply was severely threatened during the 1950s when the lamprey eel arrived in the ballast tanks of Atlantic freighters. This and man-made pollution devastated much of the Great Lakes fish population.

Third, right after World War II, something came onto the American scene that helped balance the the loss of the Great Lakes fish supply—the refrigerated truck. This vehicle's ability to keep fish frozen while traveling from coast to coast allowed cod and haddock to be trucked in to Wisconsin from the ocean.

One cook I talked with referred to this as "the reefer gladness effect" because now people in Rhinelander and Hurley could dine on fresh ocean fish. (For years, cross-country truckers have called refrigerated trucks "reefers.")

The fourth reason is truly "Wisconsin."

It is found in the mix of our background and heritage.

It is the "Germanic Imbibement Factor."

You see, back in the "old country," the whole family, children and all, went into tavern to eat and be merry. It was a family tradition.

This tradition immigrated with the family here to Wisconsin.

Other Midwestern states had "blue laws" at various enforcement levels, forbidding people of certain ages from visiting cafes, taverns, and other places where alcoholic beverages are served and consumed. Some of the states have repealed or modified their blue laws, but the concept has always been foreign in Wisconsin. The tavern has always been a "family thing" here.

To begin this journey, I went to the best source we have in Wisconsin—the people.

Wherever I traveled, while I was at the town gas station or local grocery store, I simply asked this question to people I encountered: "Where is a good place to go for fish around here?"

This is what I heard.

Our Journey Begins . . .

FIRST, A PRIMER FOR OUT-OF-STATE TRAVELERS AND TOURISTS.
A SHORT LESSON ON "HOW TO GO NATIVE" AT A FISH FRY.

Lesson 1: What to Wear to a Fish Fry

Fashion tip: All of the following items may be worn by either sex and can be purchased at any Farm and Fleet store or Cenex Gas Station. (We are not talking Mall of America or Fifth Avenue here.)

Item one: Sensible shoes. The bigger the better. The vulcanized rubber soles are ideal for waiting in line for your table or for polka dancing on sticky linoleum floors.

Item two: Big overalls. Slung low. The many pockets are ideal storage areas for toothpicks or swizzle sticks.

Item three: Tops or pullovers, anything that has a Number 4 or 92 on it. Must be green-and-gold or red-and-white. Camouflage or hunter's blaze orange is also acceptable during designated times of the culinary year. Warning: Do not wear anything that has the word "Minnesota Gopher," "Minnesota Viking," or Minnesota anything etched upon it.

Item four: Head gear. Stocking cap for winter, baseball cap for non-winter. (Fashion note: Make it a dark green stocking cap for formal events or at fancy supper clubs.)

SOREL
XXXL
4
ampions

Lesson 2: What to Say at a Fish Fry

Sprecken-zee Sheboygan?
(Or E.T.L—English as a Third Language)

(A Vocabulary Aid for Out-of-Staters)

1. UWANFRIES? (one word) Translation: "Excuse me, do you desire French fries with your cod?
2. PASSDASLAHHH! (one word) Translation: Pardon me, madam, would you please be so kind as to pass the bowl of cole slaw?
3. BRANDY OLD FASHIONED. Simply put, this is the Wisconsin State Drink. Forget milk. Got brandy?
4. UPNORT. This is a region, more of the mind than of actual geography. To someone from Chicago, Lake Geneva is UpNort. In Wisconsin the term is commonly used at the dinner table. For example, "Howie's got a cousin UpNort who got a good deal on a four by four."
5. POINT. Used in various contexts of dinner conversation. For example, used in the context of geography: "We got a deer camp just nort of Point (Stevens Point). In sports: "The Point bein', dey ain't got no runnin' game!" Or in formal occasions (such as a wedding reception or a wake): "Just Point me to the beer tent."
6. TIN. In Wisconsin, this means "thin." An example, as used in polite dinner conversation: "Hey, dere's a tin piece of cod left—who wants it?" Or, "Hey, Doris, you gettin' awful tin deese days. What are you sick or somethin'?"

7. TINK. In Wisconsin, this means "think." An example, commonly used in a sentence: "Hey, I tink dis table needs more fish here!" Or possibly, "I tink I'll have another brandy while Doris warms up the car." If Descartes had grown up in Rhinelander, he'd likely have philosophized thusly: "I tink, derefor I yam."

8. DRIVE BY. Not to be confused with an inner-city practice involving gunfire. In Wisconsin, this term is used as a parting invitation upon one's leaving a fish fry. Thus: "Hey Wally, you and da wife drive by the house sometime soon!" This is an invitation to visit the farm.

Ten Commandments of a Successful Fish Fry (Church Event)

1. Thou shall remember dates of upcoming fish fry (and commit not to forget)
2. Thou shall organize hundreds of dedicated volunteers.
3. Thou shall acknowledge the contributions of others.
4. Thou shall be patient standing in line.
5. Thou shall keep same line moving forward.
6. Thou shall not covet thy neighbor's cod.
7. Thou shall not sneeze in slaw.
8. Thou shall not mention "Minnesota Vikings" at the table (or while in attendance).
9. Thou shall not linger.
10. Thou shall give "thanks" to all involved.

A very special thank you to the members of the Ashton Fish Fry for helping write these commandments.

Brandy
Old Fashioned

The State
Drink

St. Peter's Catholic Church

"In a sense, the fish fry carries on Midwestern small town traditions of hard work, a sense of honesty, and family values still alive and practiced on a daily basis.

". . . When our fish fries take place, everyone in the family takes part in the work and effort which in turn raises funds for our school. It is nourishment for both body and soul."

—Father Bud Hollfelder
St. Peter's Catholic Church
7121 County Trunk K
Middleton 53562
Tel. 608 831-4843
Fax 608 831-5377

Fish Fries are held periodically through the year. Please call for dates.

The Stamm House

This old stone building is located on an old stagecoach trail which skirted the northern edge of Lake Mendota. It offers up an ambiance reminiscent of an old English roadhouse.

The Stamm House at Pheasant Branch
6625 Centry Avenue
Middleton 53562
Tel. 608 831-5835

STAMM HOUSE
1847
JEFF HAGEN

A PIECE OF THE NORTH COUNTRY

Five and Dime Tap

"Our place feels like a bar up North where you can enjoy good fish on a Friday night."

—Steve Quesnell, owner

Five and Ten Tap
1850 North Water Street
Milwaukee 53202
Tel. 414 272-1599

OLD STYLE
5&10
5&10 TAP

Top Ten Juke Box Hits at a Fish Fry

10. "The Bud Song." (Warning—this may cause a stampede onto the dance floor and into the parking lot.)
9. "When You Fish Upon a Bar." (This is the non-Disney version slow dance—no crickets singing on this one.)
8. "Roll Out the Barrel." polka
7. "Come Fry with Me."
6. "I'm a Sole Man."
5. "In Heaven There Is No Beer" polka.
4. "Proud Mary" (Trollin', Trollin', Trollin' on a Rrrrriver)
3. "When a Man Loves a Walleye." (A real tear jerker.)
2. "Brandy, You're a Fine Girl."
1. "The Frying Game."

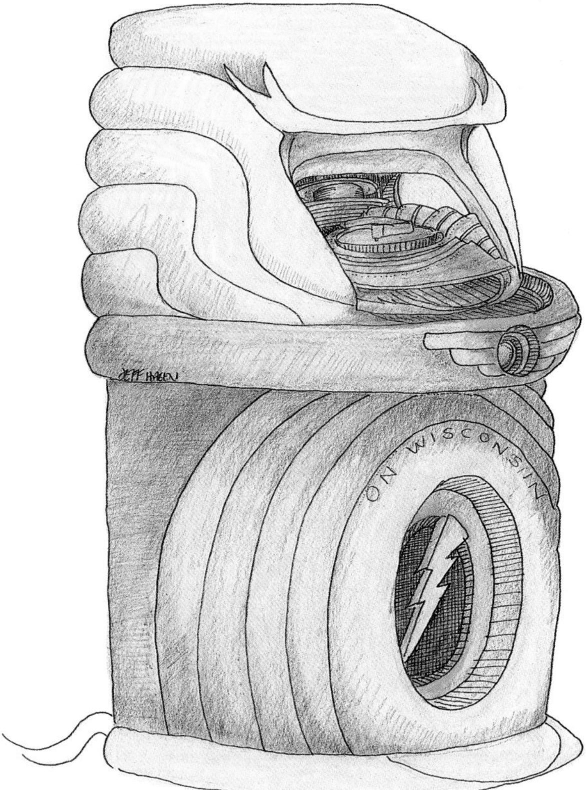
JEFF HAGEN
ON WISCONSIN

CODZILLA!

Serb Hall of South Milwaukee

This place is the largest fish fry that we attended. I was told by the people at Serb Hall that more than 4,000 people came through the fish fry on Good Friday of last year. Several of the national television networks sent out film crews to record that particular Friday here in the heartland of Wisconsin.

"This fish fry is so large that they actually have a drive-through window and a rent-a-cop directing traffic."

—J.H.

Serb Memorial Hall
(Wednesdays and Fridays)
5101 West Oklahoma Avenue
Milwaukee 53219
414 545-6030
Pictured at right: St. Sava Cathedral

JEFF HAGEN

BIG FISH IN A SMALL POND

David's Restaurant

"We still cook the old-fashioned way . . . in an atmosphere of Old World spice mixed with displayed original artwork as well as unique creations on your dinner plate."

—David Scheifel, owner and chef

David's Restaurant
909 E. Broadway
Monona 53716
Tel. 608 222-0048
Reservations required

PEPSI
DAVID'S
RESTAURANT
DAVID'S
RESTAURANT
GOLDEN
MICHELOB
DRAFT
LIGHT
OPEN
TONITE
JEFF HAGEN

8343 V.F.W. Club

Several people told me this was a good fry to visit. It is located just off the main runway of the Dane County Regional Airport, in Madison. Which, in a way, is fitting. For the first large object on the ground that appears to arriving air passengers is a Wisconsin fish fry.

8343 V.F.W. Club
Truax Longmire Post
5737 County Trunk CV
Madison 53704
608 241-3740

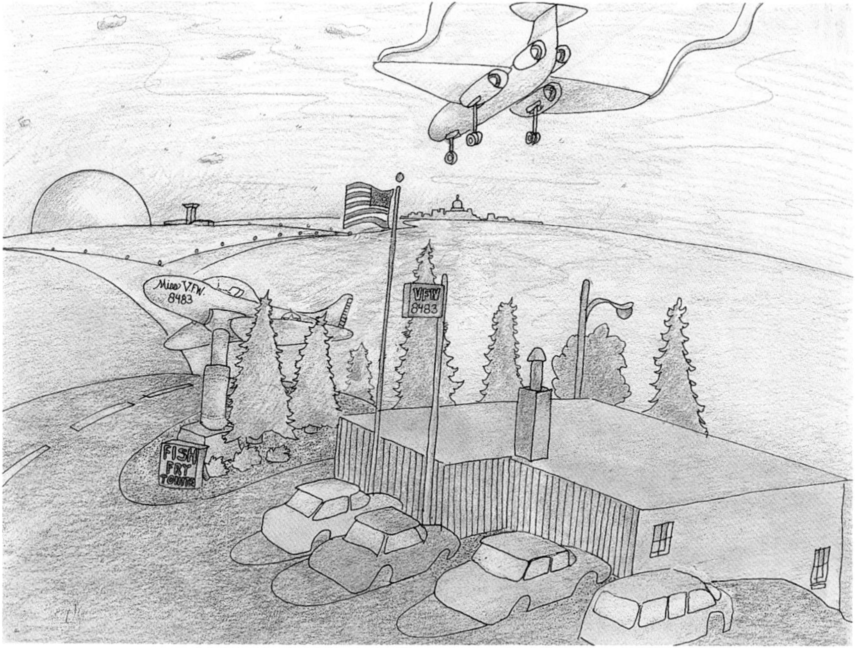
Miss V.F.W.
8483
VFW
8483
FISH
FRY
TONITE

THANK COD, IT'S FRIDAY!

The Avenue Bar

This place is a classic fish fry emporium, even though the "fry" is a fish boil, served with potatoes, carrots, and onions. It's a place where workers, business people, retirees, and university students blend in a friendly mix in common celebration of the end of a work week.

The Avenue Bar
1128 East Washington Avenue
Madison 53703
Tel. 608 257-6877

AVENUE BAR
TIMES

Pardon me, boy, is that the Wauwatosa Chew-Chew?

The Chancery

On the day that I stopped here, I picked a table right on the window side that overlooked railroad tracks just a few yards from the building. As I was looking down at the menu, a little pre-schooler sitting with his father and mother across from me jumped up and yelled, "Choo-choo!"

Sure enough, within seconds the building began to shake and a huge diesel and freight train roared by, highballing into the night.

The Chancery
7615 West State Street
Wauwatosa 53213
414 453-2300

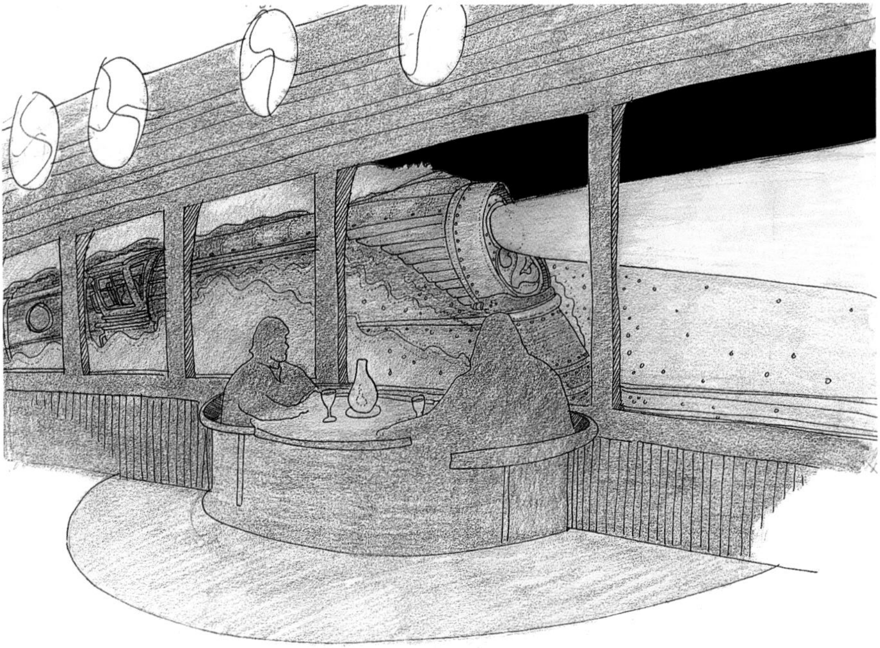

A TOUCH OF SWEDEN

Scuttlebutt's

"Our signature is great food with a great lakeside view."

—Steve Solberg, owner

Scuttlebutt's Restaurant
831 Wrigley Drive
P.O. Box 729
Lake Geneva 53147
Tel. 414 248-1111
Reservations suggested

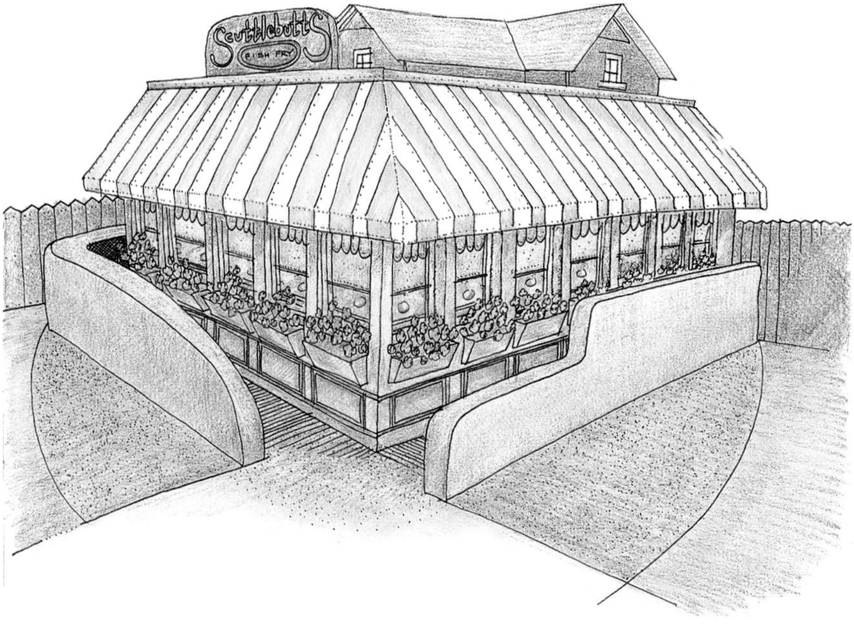
Scuttlebutts
FISH FRY

GILL-AGAINS RETREAT

The Trempealeau Hotel

If you want an alternative to deep-fried fish, this is your kind of place. One of the entrees they offer is grilled blue gills. Unique for the fact that for years it was against the law to commercially sell blue gills at eateries in Wisconsin. But now, because of commercial blue gill farms, the gills are back. The Trempealeau is also a good place to catch the blues, music offered on special nights. It's all part of the offerings in this vintage hotel on the banks of the Mississippi.

The Trempealeau Hotel
150 Main Street
Trempealeau 54661
Tel. 608 534-6898
Call for prices and specials

1891
HOTEL
CAFE
OPEN
JEFF HAGEN

FRIDAY NIGHT—DEEP IN THE HEART OF DAIRYLAND

Riha's House and Bar

"We have everyone from farmers to bagpipers who come in our place. It's a friendly atmosphere."

—Vicky Riha Gordon, owner

Riha's House and Bar
306 Main Street
Hollandale 53544
Tel. 608 967-2303

WELCOME
Riha's
HOTEL & BAR
BUD LIGHT
HOTEL & BAR
Budweiser
BUD LIGHT
OPEN

As trim as a Yankee Clipper

Trim B's

"It's a tradition here, a taste for both pallet and memory that recalls the old days when your dad cashed his weekly check on Friday evening and took the whole family out for a Friday night fish fry. That tradition still prevails here."

—Ron Tremberger, owner

Trim B's
201 Walnut St.
(Corner of Walnut and Lawrence Ave.)
Appleton 54911
Tel. 920 734-9204

TRiM B's
JEFF HAGEN

SITTIN' BY THE DOCK OF THE BAY

Mucky Duck Fish Shanty

"We make everything from scratch here. We present good food along with tender loving care to all our customers."

—Patrick and Shelly Emmer, owners

Mucky Duck Fish Shanty
701 Riverfront Drive
Sheboygan 53081
Tel. 920 457-5577
No reservations. First come, first served.

BONITA ANN
OPEN

The Old 400 Depot Cafe

This beautiful little building is a replica of the Old Town Depot that originally sat nearby in the little rail crossing of Menomonie Junction.

Back in 1935, a legend was born on the rails that passed by the old depot.

A train christened the "400" and acclaimed as the fastest train on the American continent passed through Menomonie on its daily run from the Twin Cities to Chicago. Its claim to fame was the fact that it took 400 minutes to travel 400 miles, shortening the conventional rail time between the two cities from 10 to 6.5 hours. Quite a feat in the thirties.

Nowadays, the old train is just a faded memory, but the food and service at this cafe is creating a new legend of its own.

The Old 400 Depot Cafe
2616 Hils Court
Menomonie 54751
Tel. 715 235-1993
Call for prices and specials

JEFF HAGEN
THE "400" CAPE
DEC. 28, 1998

A SIZE COMPARISON CHART

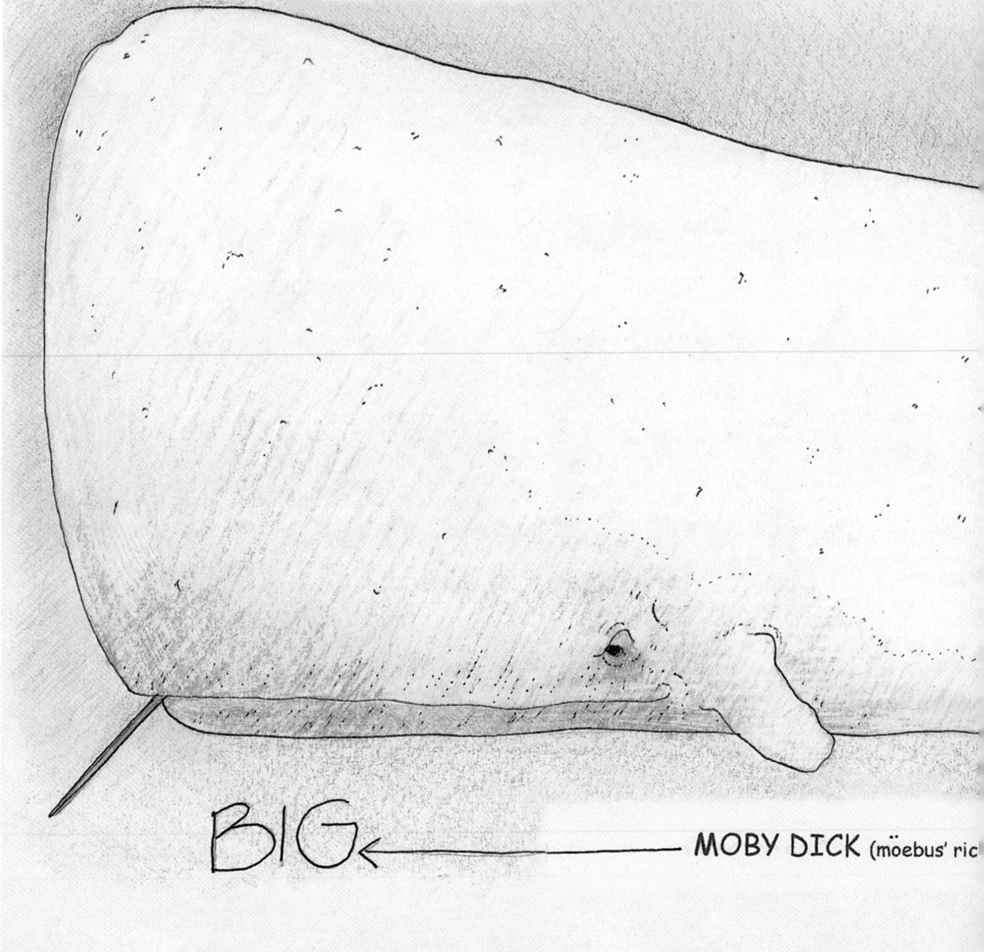

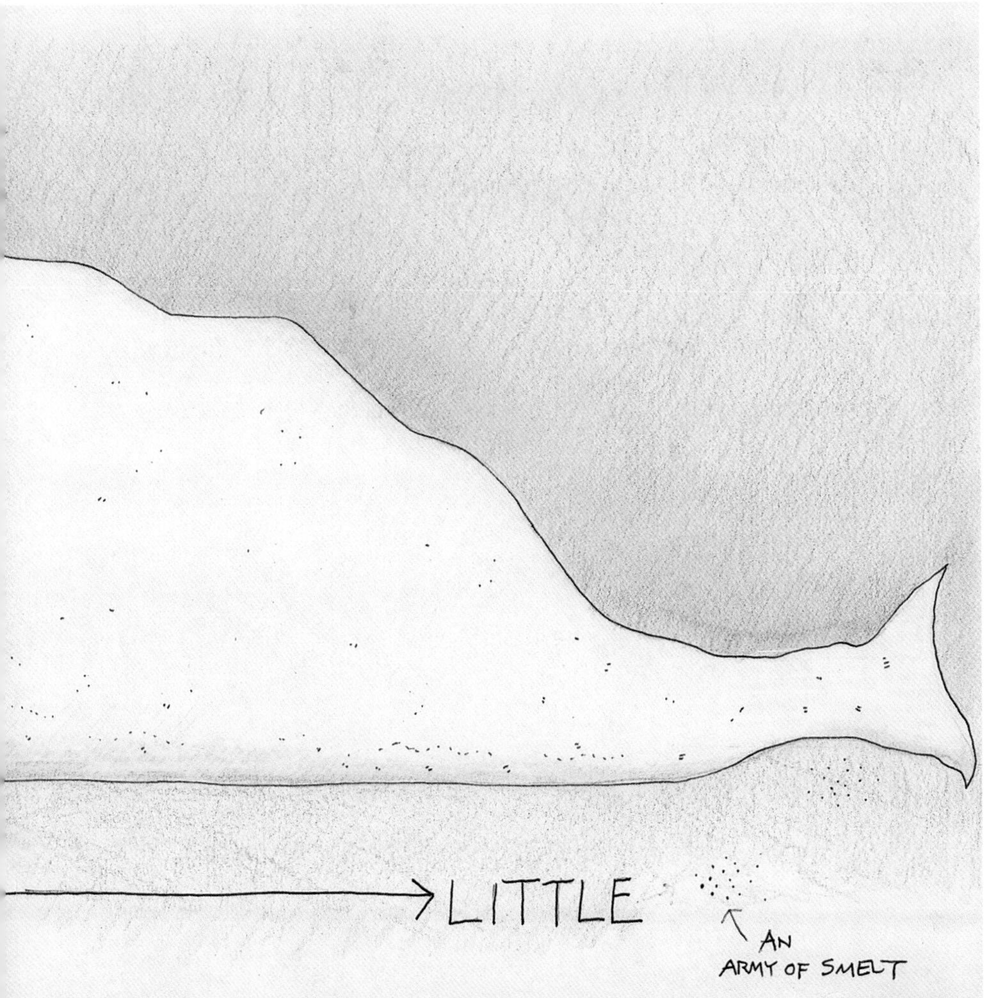
LITTLE
AN
ARMY OF SMELT

SWISS FISH

The Glarner Stube

This is a nice departure from the conventional fare of fish fries. Located in the charming Swiss village of New Glarus, the Glarner Stube offers a touch of the Old World with the new. Great fish with Roesti-fried potatoes on the side, followed by a comfortable stroll down Main Street in a quiet little village tucked away in God's Country.

The Glarner Stube
518 First Street
Box 324
New Glarus 53574
Tel. 608 527-2216

·1901 SALOMON · STUESSY 1901·
RESTAURANT
OPEN
JEFF HAMON
8·06·98

TOWN FRYER

The Town of Cornucopia's Annual Fish Fry

"It's our town's homecoming. A chance for family and friends who have moved away to come home again. The town swells to four times its size during fish fry weekend. We will go through a thousand pounds of locally caught whitefish during the event."

—Mark Ehler, town resident and fish fry volunteer

Cornucopia Club Annual Fish Fry
First Sunday in July each year
Send inquiries to
P.O. Box 113
Cornucopia 54827
Or call Ehler's Store
715 742-3232

BELL TOWN HALL

The Old Log Cabin

"When I was working for AT&T in Minneapolis, I knew some former Wisconsinites who were so diehard fish fry fanatics that they would drive back into Wisconsin at Hudson every Friday night for fish."

—Kit Hagen, best friend and beloved son

The Log Cabin
501 Sixth Street North
Hudson 54016
715 386-9499

WELCOME
OPEN

FRY ME A RIVER

Potosi Yacht Club

"People keep coming back because they know our fish fry will always be good. We have an established reputation."

—Carl and Dorothea Blindert, owners

Potosi Yacht Club
6659 Highway 133
Potosi 53820
Tel. 608 763-2238

JEFF HAGEN

Forkless in Green Bay

Maricque's

"When I first dined at Maricque's, I asked our friendly waitress for a fork. She replied, 'Oh, you must be from out of town.' This little place is both friendly and very informal."

—Bonnie Berens, fish fry fan

Maricque's
1517 University Avenue
Green Bay 54302
Tel. 920 432-9871

1517
Point
BEER
OPEN
Maricques' Bar
WELCOME

LOON STRUCK

Lost Land Lake Lodge

Hayward is a place known for fish. Where else would you find a huge walk-through muskie adorning the skyline of the town? So it's quite an honor in Hayward to be recognized as the area's best fish fry. But that's the word on the street. And that's what led me out into the surrounding lake and tall pine country to find this rustic 1930s lodge that draws up to six hundred diners on a Friday night.

The lodge rests on a pine-shaded slope overlooking a pristine lake. Soft rhythmic waves gently lap the shore, and an occasional loon serenades in the indigo night.

Lost Land Lake Lodge
9436 West Brandt Road
Hayward 54843
Tel. 715 462-3218

Local Motive

Titletown Brewing Company

"We try to redefine the fish fry in Wisconsin by offering fresh perch and cod battered with our own microbrewed beer."

Titletown Brewing Company
(Located in the old 400 Chicago Northwest Depot)
200 Dousman Street
Green Bay 54303
Tel. 920 437-BEER
Fax 920 437-BREW

TITLETOWN
BREWING CO.
GREEN BAY
400

THE HOST OF GHOST TOWN

Ghost Town Tavern

While I was pumping gas one Saturday morning in Port Washington, I asked an elderly gent in the next bay where was a good local place for fish. Within minutes, everyone at the gas station was recommending their favorite spot. It was contagious and friendly and it led us to this little corner tap with tasty fish. No ghosts, just a town that once thrived and then dwindled down to a single building left from the old community. But, judging from this tavern's food and friendliness of its customers, this sole survivor is a worthy representative of bygone days.

Ghost Town Tavern and Restaurant
I-43 & Highway 60 (Exit 92)
Grafton 53024
Tel. 414 376-9003
Call for prices and specials

OPEN
Ghost Town
Tavern
FEB 01, 1999

The Kimball Inn

"People around here prefer ocean fish rather than the local catch."

—Mike Lagalo, owner

The Kimball Inn
6622 West U.S. Highway 2
(4 miles west of the Michigan border)
Kimball 54534
Tel. 715 561-4095

KIMBALL INN
WELCOME
JEFF HAGEN

FRIDAY NIGHT WHISTLE STOP

The Silver Coach

"This place has incredible potato-crusted walleye, in a setting that is a throw-back to days of old when fine dining was the standard on American railroads."

—Jeff Hagen

The Silver Coach Restaurant
38 Park Ridge Drive
(Highway 10 East)
Stevens Point 54481
715 341-6588

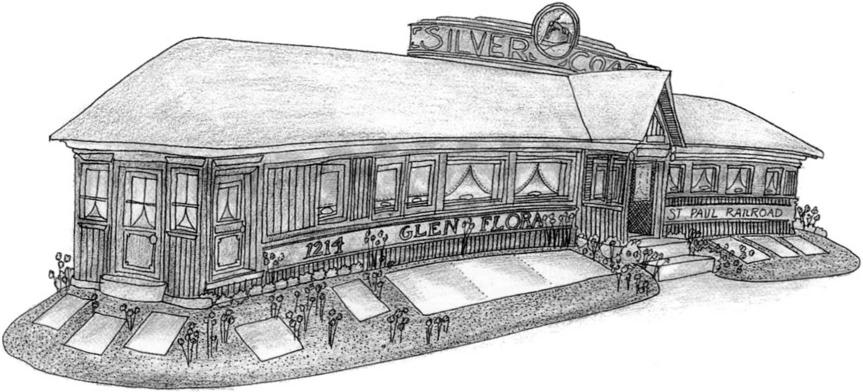
SILVER
COAC
1214 GLEN FLORA
ST PAUL RAILROAD

Mango Chutney in Paradise

Jolly Bob's

"Jolly Bob's avocado and mango chutney catfish takes you back to an island paradise."

—Tim Gingell and Judy Herman, frequent diners at Bob's

Jolly Bob's
1210 Williamson Street
Madison 53703
Tel. 608 251-3902

Jolly Bob's
jerk joint
Jolly Bob's
"wish you were here"

FISH ON A PLANK

Molly Thatcher Bar and Grill

Years ago, I taught art in the public schools of Beloit.

One of my schools was a tough inner-city elementary school that fortunately had a lively and fun-loving staff.

At the end of one very difficult school year we had a staff picnic at a park along the Rock River.

During the party, I asked one of my coworkers if they ever fished the Rock River.

"Oh, yes. In fact, I have a local recipe for you on preparing fish from the Rock. First you need to catch a good-size fish. Then clean him and nail the fish onto a wooden plank. Maple is good.

"Then you mix up a marinade of lemon, Worcester sauce, and slices of Bermuda onion. Over a period of three to four hours you slowly cook the fish, periodically basting with the marinade. When the fish turns a dark sepia color, you carefully remove the nails, throw the fish away, and eat the plank."

So, naturally, when I saw "Fish on a Plank" on the menu at the Hotel Chequemegon, I knew it had to be a joke. (After all, I had been trained in Beloit.) And so I told the waiter I was in on the joke.

After giving me a long, strange look, the waiter said, "I assure you, sir, this is no joke."

He was right. Out from the kitchen, he emerged carrying a tray with a beautiful, fresh Lake Superior whitefish on a maple plank covered with onions and sauce. It was great! A culinary delight indigenous to Gitchee Gummee country and the great wild North.

Better yet, the plank made a round-trip journey back to the kitchen.

Molly Thatcher Bar and Grill
Hotel Chequamegon
101 Lake Shore Drive West
Ashland 54806
Toll-free 800 946-5555

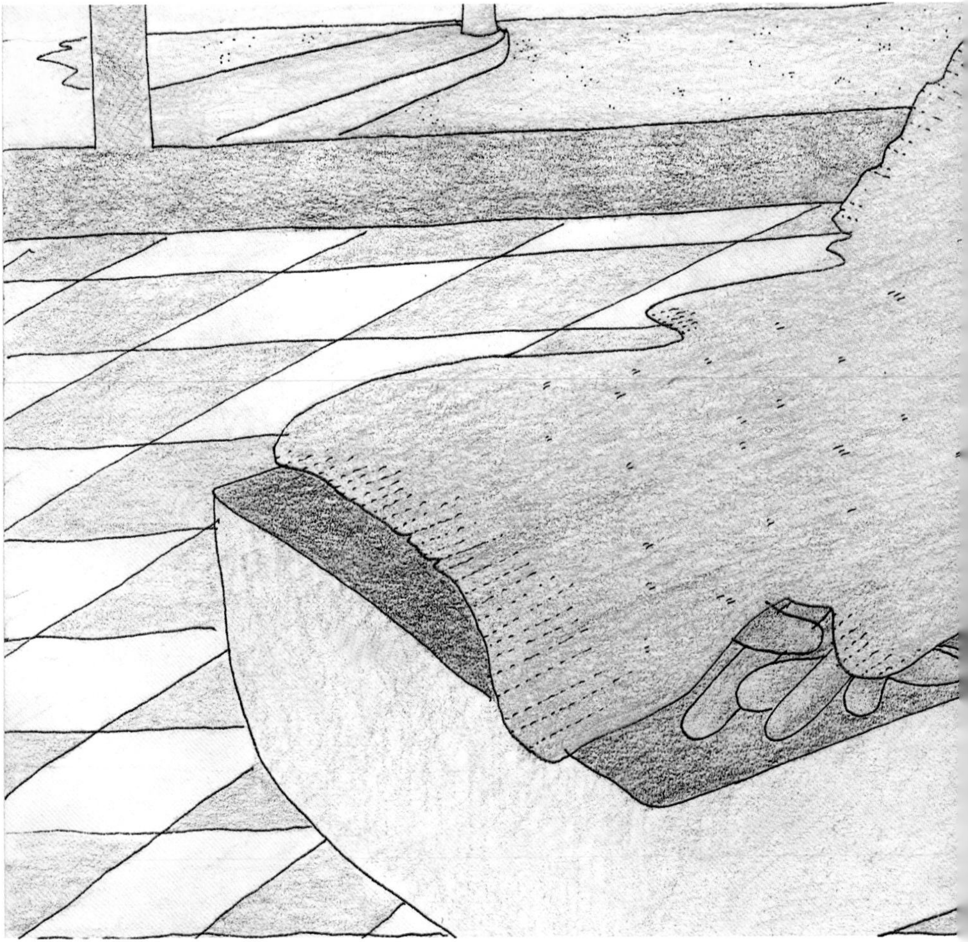

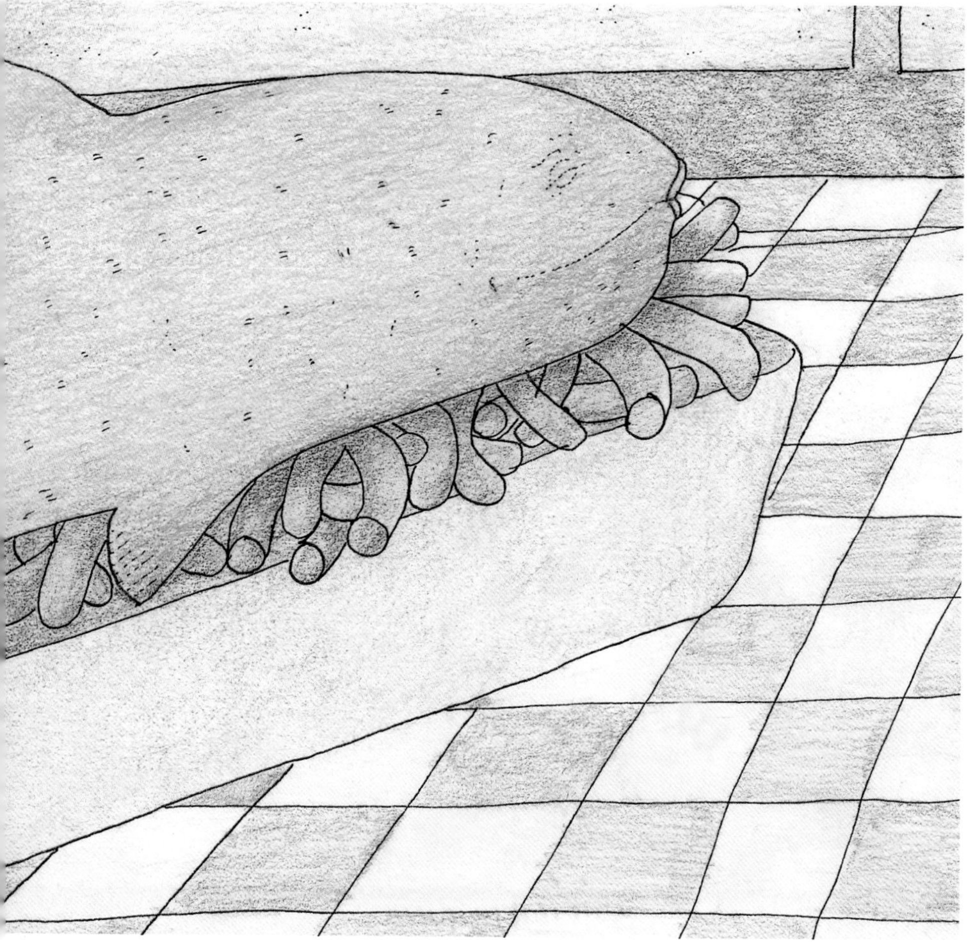

HAIL, HAIL, THE GANG'S ALL HERE . . .

Port Wing Fish Boil

For more than 30 years this little town along Lake Superior has held an annual fish boil which now attracts upwards of 2,000 people for the one-day event. The featured fish is lake trout, and as one local put it, "Once you try our fish, you'll keep coming back, year after year."

Port Wing

The annual Port Wing Fish Boil is held on the Saturday preceding Labor Day. The event is held on the town's picnic grounds on Highway 13.

THE LAST GREAT FISHING VILLAGE

The Village Inn

This is the northern most village in Wisconsin. Back in the 1940s they wanted to change the town name from Cornucopia to North Pole, Wisconsin. The decision was put to a vote and North Pole lost by a handful of votes. It is a town that once had a reputation as one of the major fishing villages on the Superior shore. Today only one commercial fishing boat pulls out of its harbor to fish. But this little corner eatery carries on that great legacy with a traditional fish boil and an extensive menu of Lake Superior fish offerings.

The Village Inn
Corner of Highway 13 and County Trunk C
P.O. Box 127
Cornucopia 54827
Tel. 715 742-3941

OPEN
OLD STYLE
OPEN
TOYOTA
GMC
FORD

Poynette

FRIDAY NIGHT SMELTDOWN

The Owl's Nest

My recollection of my first smelt trip; was back in college when we drove hundreds of miles on a dark March evening to wade into an ice-cold stream on Lake Superior. Our mission was to catch smelt.

"What kind of equipment would we need?" I asked. Beer was the answer. Lots of beer.

About 2 a.m. on a beach north of Duluth, I heard someone yell, "They're running!" So, answering the call, I waded into the glacial water with a net to "catch smelt."

I quickly learned that this is a "no skill required" activity. I wouldn't call it a sport, since the fish ran into anything that you put in the stream, including your pants!

I stumbled out of the stream with hundreds of wiggling smelt in my net and a far greater number in my jacket, sweat shirt, and throbbing blue jeans!

Aquatic vibrators, ice-cold Slim Jims. People on the beach were all doing a similar dance, shaking their pant legs and dropping out little silver fish on the frozen beach.

I decided on that cold and frozen night long ago that I would do my smeltin' indoors from then on. Some warm place where my pants stayed dry and the only beach sound came from Jan and Dean on the jukebox.

This book wouldn't be complete without a place in Dairyland that serves up a smelt fry. "Our smelt fry runs for four weeks in spring. During that time we go through a ton of smelt."

—Larry Gregor, owner

The Owl's Nest
617 North Street
Poynette 53955
Tel. 608 635-2298

Miller

OLD
STYLE

By Hook or by Nook—Low-Risk Lutefisk

The Norske Nook

To be honest, at first I resisted any urge to include lutefisk in this book. No way!

I recall a visit I took to Bergen, Norway, years ago. I was traveling on a tugboat with a Norwegian captain and his girlfriend.

After I had asked them countless questions about his home port and people, he had one question for me. "Tell me, Jeff, do people in your part of the country actually eat that junk fish?"

What could I say?

I wasn't about to defend it. It wasn't my kind of eating. So I just looked at him, befuddled, and said, "Some do, but I can't explain why."

As I researched this book, I quickly found that there is a "lutefisk lobby" out there.

I could envision their bumper sticker: "When Lutefisk is Outlawed, Only Outlaws Will Have Lutefisk."

I held out right to the end, but finally caved in and lowered the flag when I realized that this neo-Scandinavian practice is also a part of our state's fish culture and legacy.

I found a good place that serves lutefisk dinners several times a year.

The Norske Nook. The one in Osseo.

Here is a place that has a national reputation for great food, in particular their outstanding pies

So, if the lutefisk goes south on you, there is one huge consolation.

Go for the pie. You can't lose.

"We have two local guys who wait at the door for us to open. They are the unofficial local critics of lutefisk. They can't wait to try this year's batch and give us their thumbs up or thumbs down."

—Jerry Buchard, owner

Lutefisk is served several times a year at the Osseo branch.

The Norske Nook
207 West 7th Street
Osseo 54758
Tel. 715 597-3069

The Norske Nook
2900 Pioneer Avenue
Rice Lake 54868
Tel. 715 234-1733

The Norske Nook
Rice Lake branch

DOOR STOP

Sister Bay Bowl

"While you wait for your table, you can bowl a game or chat with the locals. There's always something fun to do here on a Friday night."

—Penny Anschutz, bartender

Sister Bay Bowl
504 Bay Shore Drive
Sister Bay 54234
Tel. 920 854-2841

SISTER
BAY
BOWL
SUPPER
CLUB
MAPLE
COUNTY
ZZ
OPEN
"DOOR4TOP"

A GREAT FISH BOIL, BY GULL-EEE!

The White Gull Inn

"Door County has its own twist on Wisconsin's Friday night fish event. Our special is an age-old fish boil, fired up on our maple-shaded fieldstone patio behind the inn. We take pride in serving locally caught whitefish complemented by locally grown Door County cherries. It is delicious!"

—Andy Colson, owner

The White Gull Inn
4225 Main Street
P.O. Box 160
Fish Creek 54212
Tel. 920 868-3517
Fax 920 868-2367

Up at Eddie's

Eddie's Supper Club

"We bread our fish on Fridays. It is fresh. It is the best."

—Dina Conner, owner

Eddie's Supper Club of Superior
5221 East Fourth Street
Superior 54880
Tel. 715 398-0191
Reservations required

Eddie's
OPEN

Tomahawk Lodge Resort and Supper Club

"One of our fish fry features is a North Atlantic whitefish called Cape Capensis. It is a vainness whitefish and simply delicious to eat."

—Debbie Eastwood, co-owner

Tomahawk Lodge Resort and Supper Club
N10985 County Highway CC
Tomahawk 54487
715 453-3452

WELCOME
OLD STYLE
NELLIE
ANN

END OF THE TRAIL

Hintz's North Star Lodge

"I wait all year for this! Hintz's has the best fish fry on the planet!"

—Bob Nelson, regular customer and lodge visitor

Hintz's North Star Lodge is one of the oldest resorts in the north. It was originally built as the Oliver Lodge in 1894. It was the last stop for the Chicago, Milwaukee, and St. Paul Railroad which brought in guests on Pullman cars to dine and relax in an elegant log lodge at the end of the railroad line stretching deep into the northern woods.

Hintz's North Star Lodge
Star Lake 54561
Tel. 715 542-3600
Toll-free 800 788-5215

CHICAGO, MILWAUKEE
ST. PAUL
NORTH STAR
HOTEL WALDHEIM
CODA
JEFF HAGEN
1999

The End of the Line

Hintz's North Star Lodge is the end of the line and the end of this particular journey.

Along the way I gained an appreciated knowledge about Wisconsin and its people.

I made a lot of new friends, significant friends who have enriched my spirit and soul.

As diverse as their personalities and Zip Codes are, they all shared one common denominator: a healthy sense of humor which they unselfishly shared with me.

For this gift I am extremely thankful and fortunate—to live in this great state that I call home.

—Jeff Hagen, Madison, 1999

So Many Fries . . . So Little Time

Perhaps the biggest frustration in creating this book was the fact that everyone had a favorite place for me to visit. But, in the short time I had available, I just couldn't get to them all. So here is a tip of the hat to all the people out there in Dairyland who implored me to visit: The Esquire Club, the Hilltopper, Turner Hall, Shelton's, the Elks Club of Appleton, the Granery, Mount Vernon Lutheran Lutefisk Dinner, Skylawn Supper Club, Bents Camp, the Highlander, At the Corners Supper Club, the Golf Club at Hudson, Sunnyside Resort and Tavern, Tomorrow River Supper Club, the Butterfly Club, Newport Shores, Port Hotel, the Little Bar in Belleville, the fish fry at the Catholic Church in Dane, Boobies of Milwaukee, any of the restaurants in Lake Pepin . . . and the list goes on and on.

I'll try on the next journey, in the next edition, to sit down at the table at these fine places held in high regard amongst legions of Wisconsin fish fry fans.

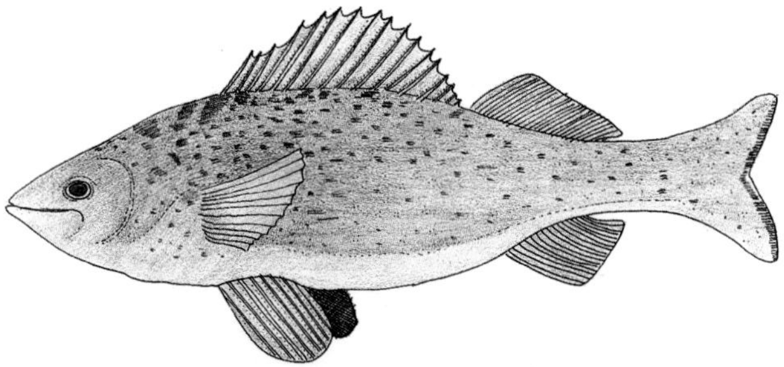

UP NORTH, IN WISCONSIN..........

IT'S WALLY........

.....AND THE BEAV..

Got Fish?

I know, I know. I probably missed your favorite fish fry place.

So, here is your chance to be in the next edition of Fry Me to the Moon. If you have a hot lead on a good place for me to visit, just clip and fax me your suggestion and we will check it out.

Fax to 608 255-4204.

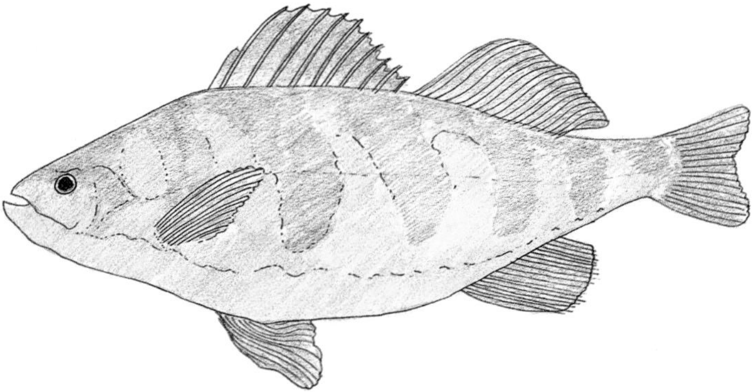

In loving memory of a great fisherman, humorist,
and dear friend

Rueben Daubner
Cornucopia
Harbormaster in Heaven

Doug Edmunds photo

About the author

Jeff Hagen is a best-selling author and artist of six published books, including two recent award winners: Steeple Chase and Hiawatha Passing. The latter was acclaimed by numerous critics, including the Minneapolis Star-Tribune, Publishers Weekly, Kirkus Reviews, N.E.A., the Junior Libary Guild of America, and the New York Times, which honored it as one of the ten best children's books in America (1995).

Jeff also writes and illustrates cover stories and travel features for many regional and national newspapers, including the Chicago Tribune, Milwaukee Journal Sentinel, Minneapolis Star-Tribune, Detroit News, Sunday Oregonian, Wisconsin State Journal, and the Capital Times, and for magazines including Cricket and Outside.

He is in frequent demand as a guest lecturer and speaker at public schools, libraries, and universities. His paintings and drawings have appeared in juried shows across the United States and Northern Europe. His artwork is part of the permanent collection of the American Embassy in Oslo, Norway.

For the past 30 years Jeff has taught art to students from kindergarten to college art. He currently teaches in the Madison, Wisconsin public school system.